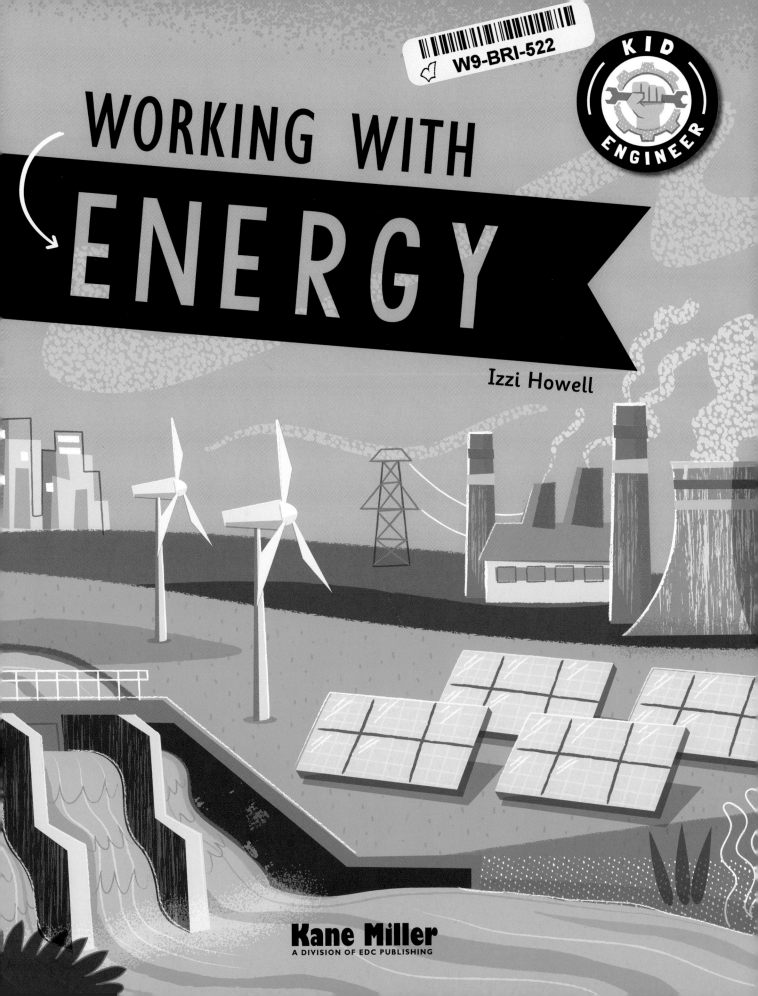

WORKING WITH
ENERGY

Izzi Howell

KID ENGINEER

Kane Miller
A DIVISION OF EDC PUBLISHING

First American Edition 2022
Kane Miller, A Division of EDC Publishing

Copyright © Hodder and Stoughton, 2020
Editor: Izzi Howell
Illustrator: Diego Vaisberg
Designer: Clare Nicholas

First published in Great Britain in 2020 by Wayland, An imprint of Hachette Children's Group, Part of The Watts Publishing Group, Carmelite House, 50 Victoria Embankment, London EC4Y 0DZ

For information contact:
Kane Miller, A Division of EDC Publishing
5402 S 122nd E Ave, Tulsa, OK 74146
www.kanemiller.com
www.myubam.com

Library of Congress Control Number: 2021937018

Printed and bound in China
1 2 3 4 5 6 7 8 9 10

ISBN: 978-1-68464-330-1

FSC
www.fsc.org

MIX
Paper from responsible sources
FSC® C144853

All the materials required for the projects in this book are available online, or from craft or hardware stores. Adult supervision should be provided when working on these projects.

CONTENTS

ENERGY ENGINEERING

Engineers design and create things to solve problems. Energy engineers design machines that turn different types of energy, such as light, heat, or movement, into electricity. They also create electrical systems.

Powering the world

Energy powers everything, from light bulbs and cars to computers and people. It makes living things and machines able to move and work. There are many different types of energy. Some examples include heat energy, light energy, sound energy, movement energy, and chemical energy.

Amazing engineers

Energy engineers need to have a good understanding of physics, chemistry, and math. They need to be curious and creative, but alert to the risks of working with electricity.

One of the biggest challenges for energy engineers today is coming up with clean, renewable ways to generate electricity to satisfy the world's rapidly growing demand. Engineers are helping to solve this problem by thinking creatively and finding alternative energy sources.

GOT IT!

American inventor Thomas Edison (1847–1931) established the first practical electric light bulb in 1879. But his invention was almost useless, as people didn't have electricity at home! So in 1880, Edison opened the first electricity company – bringing electricity to people's homes and creating a market for his new light bulb.

Energy engineers help to create systems that convert the energy from fossil fuels, the Sun, wind, and water, into the electricity we use at home and at work.

ELECTRICITY

Energy engineers design the circuits and systems that power machines and bring electricity to homes and businesses.

Current and static

There are two different types of electricity. Current electricity is generated by machines, such as wind turbines, and the chemicals inside batteries. It is sent along wires to power buildings. Static electricity is a type of electricity that exists in nature, such as lightning.

GOT IT!

Up until the 18th century, no one was sure if lightning was really a form of electricity. American scientist and engineer Benjamin Franklin (1706–1790) came up with a dangerous way of proving that it was. He flew a kite attached to a metal conductor during a thunderstorm. When Franklin put his hand near the conductor, he felt electric sparks that had traveled from the lightning down the kite!

Circuits

Current electricity flows through circuits. Circuits contain a source of electricity, such as a battery or a plug. It powers any components in the circuit, such as light bulbs or motors.

open switch

wire

battery

light bulb

This electric circuit contains a switch. When the switch is open, the circuit is incomplete, and its components don't work since the electricity can't flow. The components in the circuit only work when the switch is closed.

Conductors and insulators

Electrical engineers select materials for circuits based on whether they are conductors or insulators. Electricity can only pass through materials that are conductors, such as the metals iron, copper, and steel. Electricity can't pass through insulators, such as plastic, wood, glass, and rubber.

Engineers often choose copper, a conductor, for the inside of electrical wires. The outside is coated in insulating plastic to stop the electricity from escaping.

There's enough **electrical activity** in the **human brain** to power a light bulb!

YOU'RE THE ENGINEER:
TEST ELECTRICAL CIRCUITS

Building circuits in different ways affects the amount of electricity that reaches the components. Work as an electrical engineer and test series and parallel circuits to discover the differences between them.

You will need

Batteries
Battery packs
Wires, such as alligator
    clip wires
Light bulb holders
Light bulbs
Switches

series
circuit

parallel
circuit

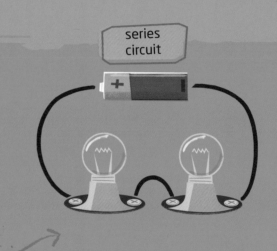

1 In a series circuit, electricity travels along one path. In a parallel circuit, electricity travels along more than one path. Build a series circuit and a parallel circuit as shown above, and test them out!

2 In a series circuit, the components share the power of the battery. In a parallel circuit, the components each receive the full amount of power from the battery. Try unscrewing one bulb in each of the circuits. What do you think will happen to the brightness of the other bulb? Test it and see.

3 A switch controls the flow of electricity through a circuit. Add a switch to your series circuit. What do you think will happen to the two light bulbs when the switch is open? Test it and see.

4 Next, add a switch to your parallel circuit. How does it affect the light bulbs? How could you redesign the parallel circuit so that one switch could control both the light bulbs?

TEST IT!

Try adding some different components to your circuit, such as a buzzer or a motor.

Test how adding more batteries affects the brightness of the light bulbs in each type of circuit. Does the position of the batteries in the circuit affect the bulbs' brightness?

Find the answer on page 31.

FOSSIL FUELS

Coal, oil, and natural gas are sources of energy. They are known as fossil fuels because they formed underground over millions of years from the remains of plants and animals.

Power plants

The key to generating electricity from fossil fuels is the steam turbine. First, fossil fuels are burned. The heat produced is used to boil water and create steam. This steam makes the steam turbine spin. The turbine then powers a generator, which produces electricity.

Going, going ...

Fossil fuels are a nonrenewable resource. They take so long to form that we will not be able to get any more once we run out. We currently use so many fossil fuels that our supply may end within the next hundred years.

GOT IT!

British/Irish engineer Sir Charles Parsons (1854–1931) designed the steam turbine as we know it today in 1884. His design was first used to generate electricity for cities. But Parsons saw that the turbine had even more potential, and, by 1897, he was using his invention to power ships!

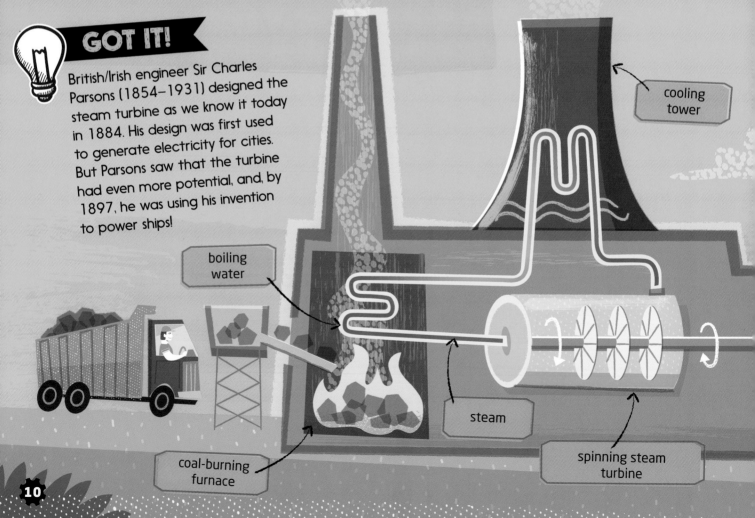

cooling tower

boiling water

coal-burning furnace

steam

spinning steam turbine

Environmental problems

Burning fossil fuels creates air pollution and gives out greenhouse gases, such as carbon dioxide. Air pollution leads to health problems and acid rain, which poisons plants and lakes. Greenhouse gases are responsible for the greenhouse effect.

Around 80% of the world's energy comes from **fossil fuels.**

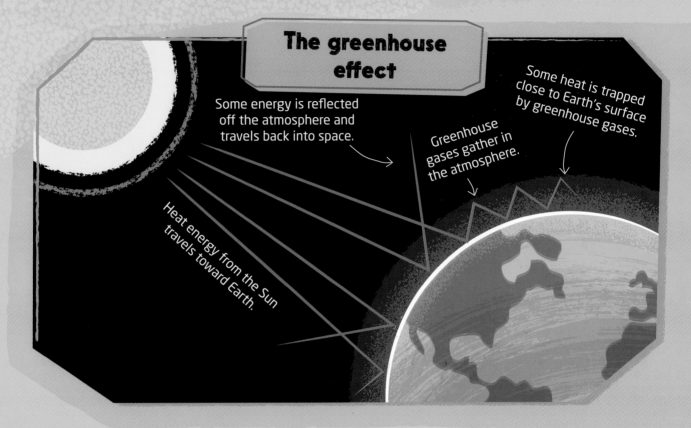

The greenhouse effect

Some energy is reflected off the atmosphere and travels back into space.

Greenhouse gases gather in the atmosphere.

Some heat is trapped close to Earth's surface by greenhouse gases.

Heat energy from the Sun travels toward Earth.

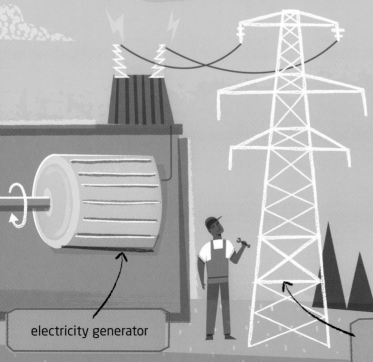

electricity generator

electricity to homes and businesses

Heating up

The greenhouse effect is making the average temperature rise on Earth. This is also known as climate change. Rising temperatures are negatively affecting some habitats, plants, animals, and humans. We need to significantly reduce our use of fossil fuels to help reduce climate change. Engineers are helping us to do so by developing sustainable sources of energy, such as wind, solar, and hydropower.

HYDROPOWER

Hydropower comes from harnessing the energy of flowing water. It has been used to power waterwheels for thousands of years. Today, engineers design hydroelectric dams to generate electricity.

Water power

Waterwheels and hydroelectric dams work in a similar way. Flowing water makes a wheel or turbine move. In a waterwheel, the wheel powers a machine for cutting wood, for example. In a hydroelectric dam, the moving turbine powers a generator, which generates electricity.

Dams and reservoirs

Hydroelectric dams are some of the largest structures in the world. When a dam is built across a river, water from the river is trapped behind the dam in a reservoir.

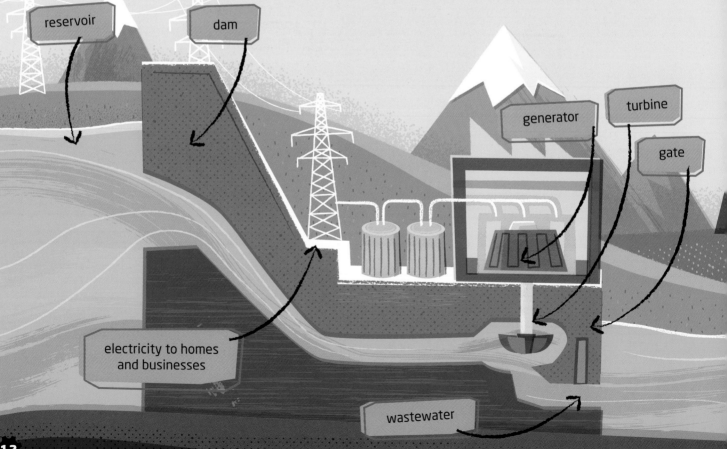

reservoir

dam

generator

turbine

gate

electricity to homes
and businesses

wastewater

Each dam structure resists the pressure of the reservoir in different ways.

force

ARCH DAM

The force of the water pressing against the dam makes the arch compress and become stronger. The weight of the dam also pushes into the ground.

BUTTRESS DAM

Buttresses (supports) built behind the dam press back and balance the force of the water. The weight of the dam also helps to keep it upright.

EMBANKMENT DAM

Embankment dams are made of layers of earth and rock. The heavy weight of the dam pushes down into the ground and resists the pressure of the water.

GOT IT!

One of the greatest engineering challenges when building a dam is moving the path of the river away from the dam construction site. In the 1930s, workers on the Hoover Dam dug huge tunnels through the canyon walls on either side of the Colorado River. The river flowed through these tunnels for five years while workers built the dam on the dry riverbed.

Today, the Colorado River flows straight through the Hoover Dam, generating enough electricity to power the homes of **1.3 million people.**

YOU'RE THE ENGINEER: BUILD A WATERWHEEL

**Put hydropower to the test by building your own waterwheel!
Lift weights with just the power of moving water.**

You will need

A 2-liter plastic bottle
Scissors
A cork
A craft knife
A metal skewer
A piece of string,
    roughly 30 cm long
A small weight, such
    as a stone
An adult to help

1 Cut the plastic bottle into three pieces using scissors. Cut the middle section into eight strips. Cut the front out of the bottom section so that water can flow out of it. (Make sure your adult helps with this, and the other steps.)

2 Use a craft knife to cut eight equally spaced slits into the cork.

3 Slot the plastic strips into the cork. The curves of the strips should all face the same direction.

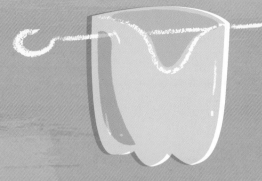

4 Use the skewer to pierce two holes on opposite sides at the top of the bottom section of the bottle.

5 Push the skewer through one hole and push the cork onto it. Then, push the skewer through the second hole.

6 Tie the string around the sharp end of the skewer. Attach the weight to the end of the string.

7 Pour water over your waterwheel. Watch how the energy generated by the wheel lifts the weight!

TEST IT!

What happens when you pour more water or make the weight heavier?

Make another waterwheel with larger strips. Compare the two waterwheels. Which one can lift more weight?

GEOTHERMAL ENERGY

Natural heat from deep underground can be harnessed by engineers as an energy source. This is known as geothermal energy.

The core is the hottest part of Earth. It can reach temperatures of 6,000 °C – as hot as the surface of the Sun!

Underground heat

Earth's core is very hot. This heat travels outward toward the surface of the planet and heats underground water and rocks. Engineers have designed systems that capture this natural heat to generate electricity and provide heating.

Capturing steam

In geothermal power plants, steam or hot water from deep underground is captured. They are used to power a steam turbine, like the ones used in fossil power plants, which generates electricity.

generator

steam

turbine

hot water

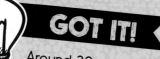
GOT IT!

Around 20 million people in Indonesia don't have access to electricity. However, there is a lot of geothermal activity under the islands, and engineers have suggested that geothermal power plants could solve this energy problem. World banks are investing billions of dollars in geothermal energy in Indonesia to increase access to electricity and reduce fossil fuel use.

Benefits

Geothermal energy has a low environmental impact. It is renewable, as the water used can be pumped back into the ground to be reheated and recycled. However, it is only possible to generate it in areas with lots of geothermal activity, such as Iceland, the US, the Philippines, and Indonesia.

electricity to homes and businesses

cooling tower

cool water

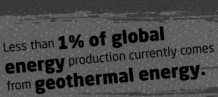
Less than **1% of global energy** production currently comes from **geothermal energy.**

WIND POWER

Engineers design wind turbines to generate electricity from the movement of the wind. Wind energy is renewable and doesn't release any air pollution, but wind farms take up space and they can be noisy and harmful to wildlife.

wind

turbine

generator

Whirring wind

Engineers have been designing wind-powered machines, such as windmills, for thousands of years. Wind turbines work in the same way as a windmill. Huge blades called sails turn in the wind and make a turbine move. The turbine powers a generator, which creates electricity.

The right place

Wind turbines need to be built in places with lots of wind, such as on mountains, or out at sea. Wind energy can be unreliable, as electricity is only generated when the wind blows. However, engineers have designed systems to store extra electricity, which can be used during periods with less wind.

sail

Downsides

Engineers are currently looking at ways to solve issues with wind turbines, such as their size, the loud noise they produce, and the danger they pose to wildlife such as birds, which are killed if they fly into a turbine's sails. Building wind turbines in areas with low bird populations helps to prevent bird deaths.

GOT IT!

The engineering firm Atkins found space to build wind turbines in a city. In their design for the Bahrain World Trade Center, which opened in 2008, they placed three turbines in the space between its two towers. The shape of the towers funnels wind to provide extra power for the turbines. They provide 10–15% of the buildings funnels wind to provide buildings' electricity.

electricity to homes and businesses

SOLAR POWER

Engineers design solar panels that gather energy from the Sun and turn it into electricity. This is known as solar power.

Special materials

Solar panels are made up of solar cells. Engineers usually make solar cells from silicon, which is a photovoltaic material. This means that it produces an electric current when it comes into contact with light.

sunlight converted into electricity

One or more

Engineers install solar panels on the roofs of some homes and businesses. The solar panels can produce enough electricity for their needs. Solar panels are also grouped together in huge solar farms. A solar farm can supply enough electricity for an entire town.

GOT IT!

It is difficult for spacecraft to carry enough fuel to power their trips through space, since fuel is heavy and takes up a lot of room. Instead, engineers design spacecraft with solar panels so that they will never run out of power!

Sunlight and clouds

Solar panels work best in areas with many hours of sunlight year round. Engineers design systems to collect and store excess electricity from solar panels so that it can be used at night and during cloudy weather.

electricity to homes and businesses

A **panda-shaped solar farm** has been built in China!

Excess electricity

Solar panels in sunny areas can generate more electricity than the building can use. Engineers connect solar panels to the general electricity supply so that any extra electricity can be sent to other buildings.

YOU'RE THE ENGINEER: MAKE A SOLAR OVEN

Work as an engineer to design and build a solar oven. Capture heat energy from the Sun and use it to cook some tasty snacks!

You will need

A cardboard shoebox
 with a lid
Scissors
Aluminum foil
Tape
A sheet of
 transparent plastic,
 such as a plastic
 sheet protector
Food
Bamboo sticks or
 pencils

1 Cut three-quarters of a rectangle out of the lid of the shoebox, leaving one side attached to the lid.

2 Fold back the rectangle and cover the bottom of it with foil, using tape to stick the foil down. The shiny side should face outward.

3 Next, cover the inside of the shoebox with foil, shiny side out.

What to cook in your solar oven?

Place a marshmallow and a square of chocolate on top of a graham cracker. Let the marshmallow and chocolate melt for a sweet treat.

Spread tomato sauce on pita bread and top with your favorite pizza toppings and grated cheese. Cook until the cheese melts to make a mini pizza.

Sprinkle grated cheese on top of tortilla chips. Melt the cheese to make nachos.

4 Cover the hole in the lid of the shoebox with the transparent plastic. Tape in place.

5 Place your food inside the oven. Close the plastic-covered part of the lid, leaving the foil-lined part propped open with bamboo sticks or pencils.

6 Leave your solar oven in direct sunlight. Check regularly to see if your food is ready.

WARNING!

Ask an adult to help with this experiment. The foil in the solar oven can get hot! Don't touch the foil when checking and removing your food. When you've finished using the oven, leave it to cool down in a shady place.

TEST IT!

What happens when you line the sides of the inside of the box with black paper? Why?

Design another solar oven using different household objects. Try using metal bowls, glass jars, or foil-lined containers.

BIOMASS

Biomass is plant or animal material that is burned to produce electricity and heat. Engineers have come up with methods of processing biomass into biofuels, which are used in vehicles and machines.

Plants to power plant

Wood, plant waste, and dried sewage (human or animal waste) are common types of biomass. Engineers design power plants in which biomass is burned to power steam turbines.

Pros and cons

Biomass is a renewable energy resource, as we can always grow more plants. However, burning biomass does release air pollution and uses up land that could be used to grow food.

Carbon dioxide is released into the atmosphere when biomass is burned.

Biomass crops absorb carbon dioxide during photosynthesis.

Burning biomass does release carbon dioxide, but this is balanced out as growing new plants for biomass removes carbon dioxide from the atmosphere. Overall, there is little impact on the greenhouse effect.

Biomass is burned to generate electricity.

Biomass is harvested and taken to power plants.

Biofuels

Liquid biofuels can be used directly in vehicles or machines, instead of gasoline or diesel fuel. Engineers create bioethanol by fermenting corn or sugarcane. Biodiesel is processed from fats, such as used cooking oil, and biogas is produced during the decomposition of natural waste.

GOT IT!

When organic waste decomposes in a landfill, it produces waste gas (mainly methane, a greenhouse gas). If this gas escapes into the atmosphere, it contributes to the greenhouse effect. However, in some places, such as the US, engineers have designed systems to collect this gas and use it as a fuel to generate electricity (see below).

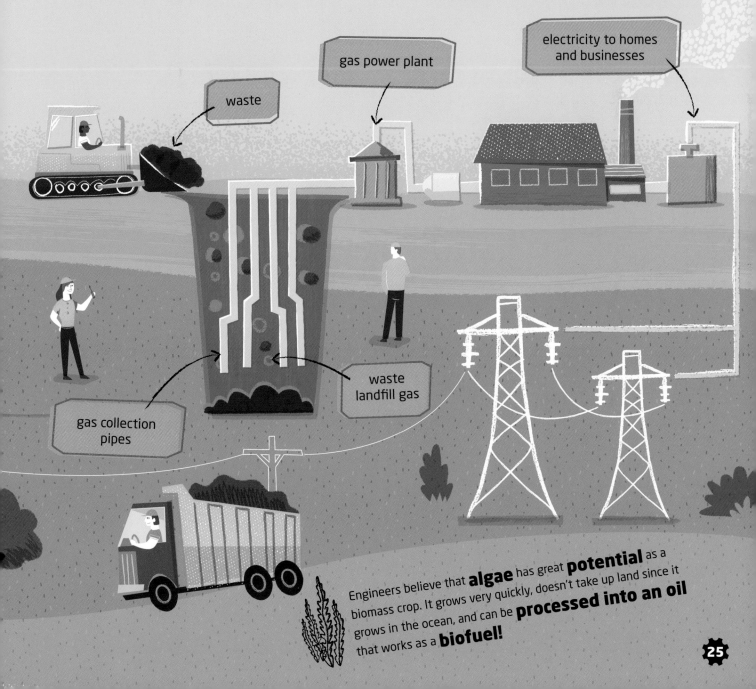

electricity to homes and businesses

gas power plant

waste

waste landfill gas

gas collection pipes

Engineers believe that **algae** has great **potential** as a biomass crop. It grows very quickly, doesn't take up land since it grows in the ocean, and can be **processed into an oil** that works as a **biofuel!**

SAVING ENERGY

Generating electricity often has a negative environmental impact, so it's important not to waste it. Engineers have developed machines and techniques to help save energy, many of which we can use at home.

Appliances

One of the easiest ways to save energy is to turn off lights and household appliances when they aren't being used. This isn't always possible, as some appliances, such as refrigerators, need to be on all the time. To solve this problem, engineers have developed energy-efficient appliances, including refrigerators, which consume less electricity than standard appliances.

Energy-efficient buildings

insulation in the walls and roof

double-glazed windows

motion sensors and timers for lights

Hot and cold

Insulating buildings is one of the best ways of saving energy. Well-insulated buildings stay warm in winter and cool in summer, so less electricity is needed for heating and air-conditioning. Engineers design new homes with double-glazed windows, draft blocks around windows and doors, and insulation in the roof and walls, and adapt existing buildings to make them more energy-efficient.

drafts blocked around windows and doors

Leaving a **computer** on overnight for a year could create enough **carbon dioxide** to fill a **double-decker bus.**

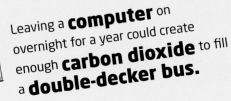

Better energy

Using clean, renewable sources of energy, instead of fossil fuels, helps to reduce damage to the environment. Some electricity companies provide electricity from green energy sources. Engineers can add solar panels or small wind turbines to buildings so that they can generate their own electricity supply.

Reduce, reuse

Consuming less and reusing objects saves a huge amount of energy, as no energy is used to extract resources, power factories, or transport goods. Recycling objects requires some energy for transportation and processing. However, the recycling process still requires less energy overall than extracting new resources.

energy-efficient light bulbs

lower the heating

energy-efficient appliances

wash clothes in cold water

reduce

reuse

recycle

YOU'RE THE ENGINEER:
TEST INSULATING MATERIALS

Insulating buildings saves energy. Work as an engineer and test different materials to find out which ones make the best insulators.

You will need

3 small paper cups
3 large paper cups that the smaller cups fit easily inside, with space around them
Aluminum foil
Cotton balls
Corrugated cardboard
Water
Books
Ice
Thermometer

1 Place either foil, cotton balls, or corrugated cardboard inside the three large paper cups. You may need to cut a circle of the cardboard to fit into the cup.

2 Place a small cup inside each of the larger cups. Fill the space around the smaller cup with the same material used at the bottom of the cup.

3 Fill each of the smaller cups halfway with water. Place the cups in the freezer and check every 15 minutes until the water has frozen solid.

4 Remove the cups from the freezer. Place them on a baking sheet. Put a book on top of each of the cups to stop them from moving around.

5 Ask an adult to help you boil water. When the water has boiled, ask the adult to pour the water into the baking sheet around the cups.

WARNING!

Don't touch the equipment or the boiled water. Do not clean up the experiment until the water has totally cooled.

6 Check your cups every few minutes to see which one melts first, second, and third. Which material slows down the melting process best and is therefore the best insulator?

TEST IT!

Repeat the experiment with other materials. Are they better or worse insulators than the materials that you have already tested?

Reverse the experiment by using hot water inside the small cups and filling the baking sheet with ice. Use a thermometer to test how quickly the water in each cup cools down. Are your results the same?

GLOSSARY

biofuel fuel produced from plant material

biomass plants, wood, or animal waste used as fuel

circuit a system for creating electricity containing wires, batteries, and components

component the name for one of the parts of a circuit

conductor a material that electricity or heat can pass through

decompose to break down

energy-efficient describes something that doesn't use much electricity or fuel

extract to take something out

ferment when sugar in a substance turns into alcohol

fossil fuel a fuel that comes from the ground, such as coal, oil, or gas

generator a machine that makes electricity

geothermal energy energy that comes from heat underground

greenhouse effect the effect when certain gases gather in Earth's atmosphere, trapping the Sun's heat close to Earth's surface and making it warmer

greenhouse gas a gas that traps heat in the atmosphere, such as carbon dioxide

insulate to cover something with a material to stop heat or electricity escaping or entering

insulator a material that electricity or heat can't pass through

landfill a place where trash is buried in the ground

nonrenewable describes something that can't be reproduced and can run out

parallel circuit a circuit in which electricity travels along more than one path

renewable describes something that can be reproduced and will not run out

series circuit a circuit in which electricity travels along one path

solar farm a place with lots of solar panels in the same location

turbine a machine that produces power by using something to turn a wheel

INDEX

ANSWER

To create a parallel circuit where one switch controls both light bulbs, the switch would need to go in this position.

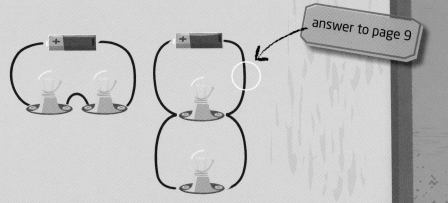

answer to page 9

COLLECT THEM ALL!